A Companion

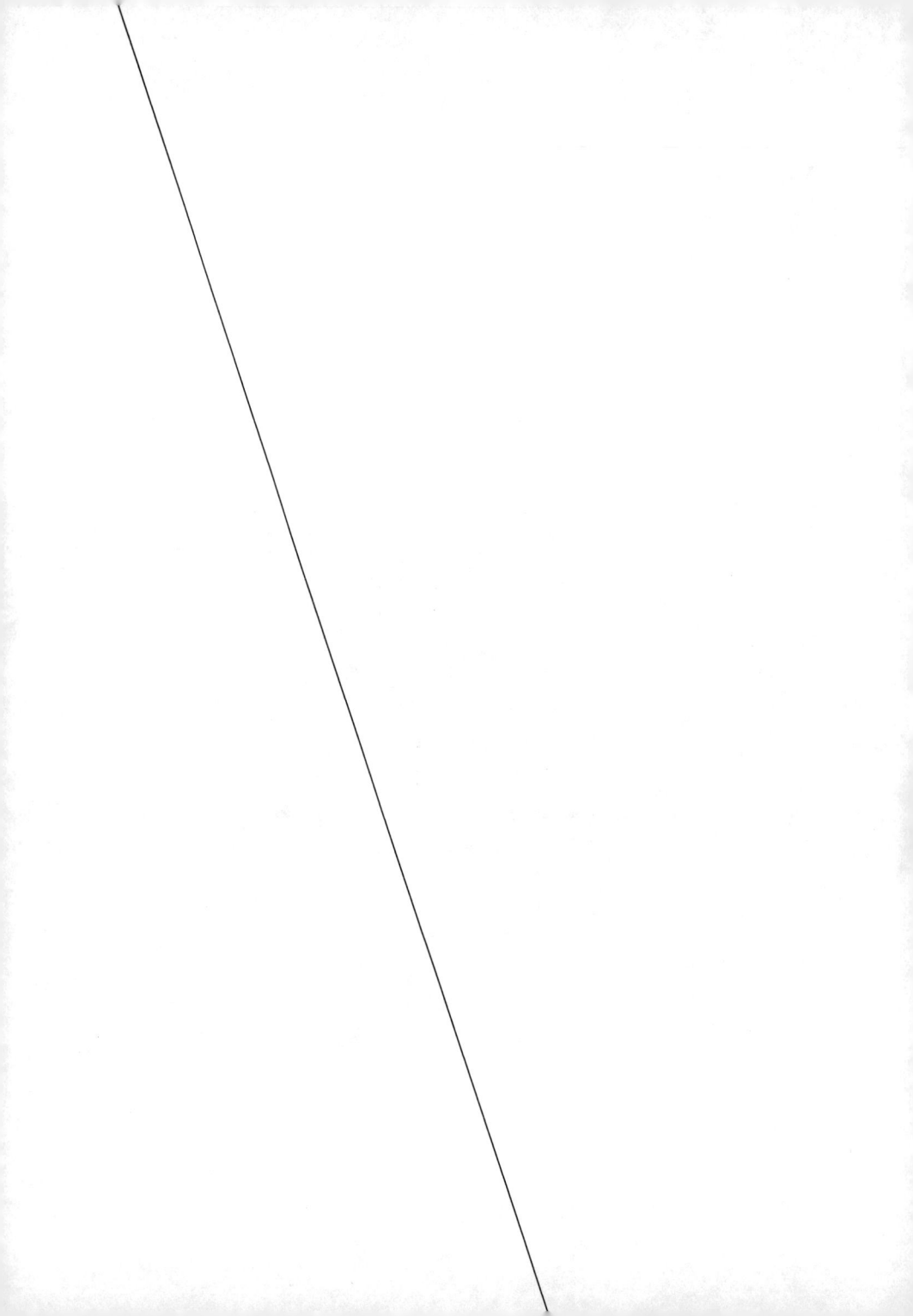

A Companion

Wave Books

Seattle/New York

Richard Meier

Published by Wave Books
www.wavepoetry.com
Copyright © 2025 by Richard Meier
All rights reserved
Wave Books titles are distributed to the trade by
Consortium Book Sales and Distribution
Phone: 800-283-3572 / SAN 631-760X
Library of Congress Cataloging-in-Publication Data
Names: Meier, Richard, 1966– author.
Title: A companion / Richard Meier.
Description: First edition. | Seattle : Wave Books, [2025]
Identifiers: LCCN 2024038721 | ISBN 9798891060159 (paperback)
Subjects: LCGFT: Prose poems.
Classification: LCC PS3563.E3459 C66 2025 | DDC 811/.6—dc23/eng/20240913
LC record available at https://lccn.loc.gov/2024038721
Designed by Crisis
Printed in the United States of America
9 8 7 6 5 4 3 2 1
First Edition
Wave Books 124

"One of those open fields . . . shaped like ears"	3
An ideogram for our descent thus far	11
An indefinite and expanding time	23
the other cast	39
Thickening	57
"And"	67
Cia ao ao ao ao ao ao	85

"One of those open fields . . . shaped like ears"

The catbird squawking on the peak of the garage flies down and continues on the grape vine six feet from me then plucks a green grape, holds in its wide-open beak for a beat, then swallows in a single gulp, its throat bulging out hemispherically as the grape passes through, after which, with a final squawk, it flies away

as I begin to think yesterday Chuck said hackberry and I remembered it was the word I meant to use when I wrote *hack bush*, feeling, as so often, I was wrong in a way that contained something connected to the truth. At 9:27 p.m. last night we ran out to the park along

Lake Monona to watch the moon rise and were blinded at first sight by a pair of orange lights shining out toward us but also down and into the water, trailed on either side by

blue lights spaced along the gunwales of what we took to be a police boat and the men on the bow peering down into the illuminated water to be searching for a body until we saw they held compound bows, arrows nocked, attached to lines ready to play out, and realized the bodies

they were seeking in the water were the living ones of fish. James said one man had shot as we watched and pulled in a small fish pierced through the center. When my eyes cleared and adjusted to the dark, the boat had gone up the river and I saw no moon but pointed out a small rectangle of orange lights with a curved top radiating the same color between a stand of trees, a bit darker than the sky, and the dim façades of the small apartment buildings that line the east side of the lake. We took it for another building under construction lit with the glow of high-pressure sodium-vapor lamps that allow round-the-clock labor, but as we studied it and tried to determine finally what it was, it began to ascend slowly, yet faster than a structure, in two minutes clearing

the horizon and the trees and buildings that had acted as a partial screen, leaving only the top right crescent of the otherwise bright orange circle in darkness, and we felt ourselves, in the kind of mental sensation that reaches down to the fingertips and toes, on the surface of the planet turning toward it, while the sun hung in space to our left and below our feet, shining up on the moon. The catbird, returning and this time landing on the railing of the small back porch less than an arm's length from my face, a moment ago but faster than I can write, has fled with a squawk of surprise such as we might have uttered had we its voice when the surface of the planet began to tilt and roll toward the moon. Another unseen and unknown bird

begins to whistle. I take it for James, who does the same in the morning, to signal that he is awake and to listen for an answer.

We have often noted that inside the house noises from the driveway, street, sidewalk, trees, even the interior of the neighbor's house seem to be part of our interior, their source just outside the door to the bedroom, on the stairs, or in the basement, and outside, I was now learning, it seems the reverse is also true. As I paused before finishing that sentence, a squirrel

with a nut in its mouth, of the same sort we found in the Yellow River State Forest to have the sweet astringent odor of a walnut liqueur, ascended the steps and then, so still was I sitting without intention as I waited for the next word, hopped onto the black-walnut log standing at my feet. We'd brought it back from Wyalusing State Park, after receiving permission from a man in a pickup when he stopped to speak to us as we inspected the logs piled

along the edge of an unused parking lot. The man explained they were from trees he and his men had cleared from the trails in the park, among the hundreds that had fallen in a big storm earlier in the summer, and we were welcome to take them, as far as he knew. I noticed then he wasn't a park ranger, as I had assumed. A patch above his left shirt pocket read *Corrections Officer*. We thanked him and as he drove slowly away we nodded and smiled at the men in the back of the truck, who seemed mildly surprised to be so greeted but responded in kind and their orange T-shirts, as if it were the shirts and the men rather than our slow perceptions that were changing, became prisoners' uniforms, printed with the letters *PDC*, and our greeting became one that was crossing a divide that normally prevented even this small communication, a divide that stayed with me as we walked down into the hollows toward Sand Cave and Little Sand Cave, reminded by the steep banks, the space between the trees, and the dry stream beds of the forest behind Fort Bragg, California, where we'd passed another group of men imprisoned by the state, in orange jumpsuits, clearing the dirt fire road where we entered the forest before

parking and hiking to one of the last groves of old-growth redwoods in that area, giving rise to the sensation, another mental sensation become physical, that was in fact physical, as had happened to us on the earth as it turned us toward the moon, that the paths and trails in all the forests we walked were cleared by imprisoned men in orange shirts or jumpsuits, whom we rarely saw and then were allowed to greet only silently. Wordsworth in Wordsworth's poem, suddenly stopping his line of motion, sees the cliffs wheel by him, as if Earth's motion were suddenly visible in his error,

an experience repeated as he faces the drowned man and feels the skin of the corpse through the wet clothes that cling to it, though he had only looked, and from a distance, and also experiences in his body the hanged man turning on the gallows, though he'd long since been buried, as the wind that later ruffles the clothes of a serving girl touches him, to none of whom he is otherwise

able to speak. The squirrel looked around nervously, it seemed, from its perch three feet away, turning the nut it held with the motions of its mouth alone, so it rotated like a tiny moon, while I wondered if it could, as is true of deer and other creatures, see me to be living only if I moved. In a mix of fear and compassion I can't untangle, I flexed my fingers in a slight wave, at which its eyes bulged and it leapt off the black-walnut log and bounded

down the stairs, retreating to the far side of the driveway where it chewed through the nut it hadn't dropped and ate the kernel inside, leaving the husk behind as it scampered off, leaving me searching "all round for my lost guide," whom I had forgotten and, as I finished my writing, hoped would soon wake.

An ideogram for our descent thus far

How do you go down into the valley? Walking on an animal path through the leaves, pushing aside the branches floating over the stream that is open to the running water below it, in the realization the water is below the stream, visible here where the surface is an overlapping and ingrown meshing of rectangular white ice crystals three feet from a pocket open to the forest canopy of bare branches, an opening that appeared again by a fallen tree, where the stream turned south against the sandy bank and this plunge into the tiny structures

at our feet corkscrewed around into something larger than going down we had imagined. Several others cross the stream first, looking for a way across, and then a third climbs the hill in front of me, and I take the lead by following. A bench seen through the leaves, though we have been walking away from the neighborhood and road, toward flood plain, river, and field, has at its base a gravel path and the memory I had this afternoon as I wrote of driving on a dark road into a valley which, as I was unable to call into being the beginning or ending or name of the place, became a kind of loop, replaying in my

mind so it seemed to go on and on, the negative image of the glimpse of stream that seemed always to start over as the eye flickered back and forth trying to track its course, a sensation I've received countless times in study of fast-moving water, with a history that matched each of its iterations and the objects of its attention. The gravel path, covered in ice beside the bare leaves, descended again, into another valley, a wetland like the first, but larger, with a stand of reeds, and a small river into which the first stream flowed, becoming a tributary, as the awareness of the arrangement of the landscape the further one goes into it sometimes becomes, as this one had, a bird's-eye view projected out from a low center. The graffiti under the railroad bridge over the river appears freshly

painted in red, yellow, blue, and white. Again there is ice and an air space below it, larger than the last, where the water collides with the bank and turns south. The movement of the people, a step toward the ice, two steps north to examine a hole in a tree, squatting down to see that the lines in the silt are the impressions of bits of grass since departed from the fine, ashy-gray soil, gives the appearance of looping while in fact moving forward, at every moment replaced by a new group of people making nearly identical movements, as impossible to return to as the water in the stream, an impression confirmed by senses of rightness, strangeness and déjà vu triggered by the sudden return to the present after a lapse in consciousness so brief one is aware of it only in the peculiar familiarity of the scene, caused by its reappearance on the other side of a void. These impressions were confirmed for me by the return of isolated moments, seen as through holes punched or eroded in a solid surface: the car descending,

as I mentioned, into a valley; the rusting farm implements that appeared only once in a meadow long since covered over by houses arranged around Federal Eagle Road, a cul-de-sac curved to divide all available space in the woods and meadows into lots; the forking paths in a wood in France that left the lost walker forcing himself (and I was he) through a hedge, from which I emerged bloodied at the base of a column of smoke pouring from the chimney of a house in a small settlement from which a kind couple stepped out the door, nodding and smiling at my wonder and fear as one does for a child, and drove me 20 kilometers around the woods that seemed to flicker for hours before the small château where a friend had rented a room for the weekend and from which I'd set out appeared; but also a tile dump below a stand of pines on the Italian coast from which several unbroken tiles had been brought home in a

backpack; and a closet stumbled into while asleep, the sleepwalker trying to find the red light of the stage seen in a dream and seen again on waking in the form of a fire engine's siren lights outside his bedroom window; and the moment when a rock, really a massive, sharp-edged chunk of torn-out sidewalk disposed of along the bluff as a buffer against the lake, shifted suddenly and left me with a vivid memory, isolated by the gap or void the subsequent impact left behind it, of lying in the air looking out at the water, an effect that joins all these moments and leaves me to wonder what, in the absence of trauma, erased all context from scenes that remain as vivid and detached as the graffiti,

bright, protected, and illegible, in the grotto made by the stone supports of the railroad bridge. I was reminded of a scene from *Green Henry (Der grüne Heinrich)* by Gottfried Keller. I'd finished reading a translation (A. M. Holt) of the novel five years before, near the beginning of my current project, though at a time many of the aspects of it, including a direct involvement in the theater, had yet to appear. In the scenes from the novel that now return to me, Schiller's play *William Tell* is acted across several villages and mountains, forests and rivers, by all the people of the region and Green Henry, so called because of the suit of green clothes he wears daily as a boy in the opening chapters, is part of the play and also not part of it, as I remembered, but the proceedings are so vast and intermingled, over the course of a day and night, with the life of the valley, the villages on either side of it, one sitting on the slope of the mountains, the other in the river valley, that I can't tell without the book whether the decision to abandon his role registers on his surroundings, which begin to include me, or even registers with him, as he continues to note what is going on around him—wagons, sheep, a father and son, a robber, trees and rivers and clouds and

mountains—which are what constitute the story, of the play, the novel, and the villages. I felt something similar as part of a crowd sleepily disembarking from a plane after a night flight and proceeding through a series of windowless corridors, perhaps a dream I am having on the plane I pretended as I walked, as if I were beginning to wake up but hadn't quite, as the corridors turned right or left every 20 or 30 meters, a maze whose arrows led us to a locked glass door that rattled in the hand of the first of us who reached it and pulled sharply on the handle, expecting it to open, beyond which we could see the signs for Customs, EU Nationals, and All Others, and yet more arrows pointing to the rows made by the ropes and stanchions meant to organize those arriving, then a long row of high windows, each sealed with plexiglass except for a small curved opening, through which documents could pass, in all of which

not a single person, traveler or official, stood. The sound of a train made me stay our motions. One boy (or so he seemed to me) in our dozen also heard it, but the rest continued wandering to and fro or standing very still, swaying a little from side to side, while he and I listened, alternately glancing at the track or staring at the ground below us, studying which seemed to allow me to hear better. That was when I saw what the grass had written in the silt of the bank. Ten minutes later, realizing the train wasn't going to come, we gave up and moved on. To the north, a side path had been trampled through the long winter grasses. On each straw-colored stalk, two leaves flopped on either side of the sharp tip. The path continued over a chain-link fence that had been bent down so far the snow and grasses came up through the links, though five feet further on it ended where the curling wires were nailed to the trunk of a willow. To the south, among the wetland grasses and bright red dogwood in the center of the meadow that was also a flood plain, I pointed out a shrub with bright yellow branches of fall growth standing alone. On the north side of the path, where the fence had been, a vine wound

around and over the several trunks of a wild cherry. A dozen steps farther on, hard to distinguish at first from the tangle of vines, brambles, and branches, a pair of deer legs, stripped of fur and flesh, were balanced over a branch at head height, as if the creature were kneeling in the air. As I stood and looked at the bones, after a moment I noticed, closer to me, a pelvic bone and five vertebrae dangling down, turning a little in the breeze. As my companions speculated that an animal may have dragged the carcass into a tree to eat it, I pointed to the length of wild grape vine threaded through the pelvic girdle and woven into a circle around a thin branch from which the conglomeration hung. Then, before the brief ascent up the icy path back to the ridge, I saw the body of a moth in the path. As I bent over to look more closely, it proved to be a delicate pair of vertebrae, from which two tiny ribs extended in either direction, reminding me, even as I saw it wasn't an insect, of the cicada I'd seen two summers before on a gravel path at the

outermost edge of one of the banlieues in Marseille, a valley of sorts bordered by an hypermarché, a prison, a water treatment plant, and the fantastically sharp and steep ridges that led me to the calanques and the sea. It was the only time I saw the body of one of those creatures, whose sounds accompanied me on all my walks in that region, a body so light it seemed to be filled with air. A fine layer of white-gray dust, blown from where the maquis had been cut into for some abandoned building project and a dusty figure eight had been inscribed by the scooters the local boys rode around and around in a perpetual sideways, sliding skid, a technique known as dérive or drift, covered it. The vertebrae and ribs must have belonged to a rabbit or squirrel, or the bird whose gray and white feather I saw when I was released from my vision and began to walk again. It turns out there is another play that stages the whole town in *Green Henry (Der grüne Heinrich)*. Searching, as I do, from the back toward the front, I came upon the second and forgotten play first, a carnival play in which the people of an Italian city take on roles from the town's history. The role I noted, first for itself and then as one that was clearly not part of *William Tell*, the play for which I was searching, was the fool of the Emperor, a wise fool as the narrator, Green Henry, tells us, and one who is "not so much a poet as, in himself, a poem." Green Henry is also a fool in the play, a quiet one, as he says is his nature, and, looking back at these fragments, remembering that later the

two fools fight, I thought it must be the quiet poet who sets himself to silence his noisy poem, or else the poem itself that defeats the quiet poet. But returning to the novel I thought instead of two stones, one of ice and one of rock, that the waves had thrown together and left almost touching on the shore below the Beach Aire Motel, as I read the chapter's end: "I dreamed that I had stabbed my friend dead, but that instead of him, I myself was bleeding, and was being bandaged up by my weeping mother. Meanwhile,

I was struggling with dream sobs, which awoke me." The brass horse, a copy of one found in a Chinese tomb, with tiny wings traced like distant thunderbolts along his shoulders, one of which the horse looked over on the yellow desk, peering around the corner of a stone, as it had on the table at the motel, faced the porcelain sea otter, given to me as a symbol of myself. Modeled as she was, floating on her back, hands folded on her belly, chin resting on her chest, I was struck by how the two figures had almost the same shape: the horse's chin resting on the spine, the otter's on its chest, as if who was staring ahead and who was looking back was not apparent in things

seen from even a slight distance, and I wondered how clearly the sea otters we saw off the Santa Cruz coast, floating in the kelp beds with pups balanced on their stomachs to nurse, saw us, who were also floating, despite showing no interest in our gaze at all. The two carnival plays appeared to me again in the insect tracks, first mentioned by Nycole at the railroad bridge, so that when we looped back and I saw them as we ascended toward the ridge, I felt it was already the second time. I saw the tracks on the inner side of the bark lying in the leaves, and then in the body of the log. Both seemed at first to be a map of our walk, then the original of the ghost maps of the Lower Pecatonica, printed on the pages below the sketch as the ink was drawn through them by the water of the river, and finally the map Borges had imagined in one of his stories, a map of those lives at a one-to-one scale. I intend soon to return to the path toward the ridge with charcoal and newsprint to transfer the maps to paper from the body of the log and the inner side of the bark by taking, as we were forbidden to do on the faces of the gravestones at the local cemetery, a rubbing of the grooves.

An indefinite and expanding time

Sitting in a circle with people, we're taking turns pulling a roasted carrot or potato from a bowl and each has a message, some indicating the death of the chooser. I choose one with my eyes closed. I expect a carrot, but a potato stares back. It's cut in half and the white flesh has a brown spot at the center that suggests an eye. Everyone is asking what it says and I can see words but I don't say them. Instead I say, "I'm having a vivid memory

of a fear I had as a child. Certain thoughts couldn't be escaped once you had them. They drew you in deeper and deeper and if you couldn't escape the thought, that was death. And the memory of the thought was a sensation, of lines inscribed in a bowl that turned out to be a funnel, with a black hole at the center." Attempting to explain this to my companions I added, "It's one of those dreams in which you wake up and explain the dream you just had, but that is another

dream, the dream of explaining. And then on waking up from the dream of explaining, you explain the double dream, but then that is a dream also, a third dream, the dream with the feeling of an indefinite and expanding time, and when the night is finally over, whoever he was who had those dreams is gone." She, the dog crying to be touched, licks the word

falls in the phrase *falls out of one's own mouth, spit glistening on the threads*, while I sit on a high stool facing the workbench I'd dragged out of the dumpster at a local school and carried home over the pedestrian bridge. A juniper trunk balances between my legs and the bench. I am gouging out the space where the trunk divided into two trunks a foot or so above where it had emerged from the soil and the roots it was

cut off from by a neighbor who left it on the sidewalk, within sight of its stump, to be picked up by the Department of Public Works, an event which I prevented by carrying it home as I had the bench months earlier, before either could be disposed of, the bench in the landfill, the log at the chipping yard, where it would have been ground very quickly into chips like the ones I gouge away very slowly, a difference in

pace that exists in anticipation of the other difference, the primary difference, the difference I don't know yet, a difference before the trunk is indistinguishable from thousands of letters, after it has become visible in its underlying structure, the slight angle at the crotch that produced more and more space between the tips even as it forced them together where the split had originated. The degenerate points so enclosed left me

wandering in one or two or three entities the lines made into sentences and paragraphs. I want to be under a big green tree, a girl says and her grandfather points, before he spreads the blanket in the grass, to the crown of the cottonwood so large and high that

looking up I no longer see the trunk and along with the girl doubt
that beneath a big green tree is where we are. Another girl,
running in circles on a trampoline, smaller than the boy and girl
chasing her, shouts as she falls,

I quit, you can't touch me. C. would tell here the story of tipping
D. off the edge of the boat, how in that time he told himself it was
an accident, that he was just horsing around. He would describe
how D.'s head went right by the propeller, as if his head was inside
D.'s head in that moment, the moment he told it and the moment it
happened. 40 years later D. died suddenly, of

cirrhosis of the liver or complications from Covid-19. C. always
had exceptional balance, W. would say, and had always been able
to throw people off balance from that place, as if C., in asking why
he had thrown D. off the boat, had actually been asking how, as if
to know how was a comfort. *The Tree of Gnosis* on the bookshelf

below the rich blue water of the metal globe, then all the waves
of grief (including the one on the breakwater in Cassis when I
looked up into the sea wave before it landed on me) met me at the
conclusions and folded back

so the tree almost touches them and in the little gap between the
person appears and I decide to stop and eat the apple the man at
the fruit stand washed the dust off of without a word, seeing I was

setting out on a walk, just before the prison, where people waited that Saturday outside the 20-foot-tall steel door with plaid sacs de rangement of food and laundry for those held within, and the path to the mountain that today is, exactly a year later, a loop

around a flat hot town where, covered from head to toe against the sun, I'm walking on the long side of a construction site for years a vacant lot meadow across from another lot that still is full of clover, coneflowers, and thistle as a white wrapper or light paper, rolled by the wind on its long axis, joins the page from last year blown across the roundabout between the hypermarché and the public housing, last dwellings before the cliffs rise and fall to the Calanque de Sormiou and the two places map

onto one another, and also a third, Hokusai's *Ejiri in Suruga Province*, and a fourth, Jeff Wall's photograph *A Sudden Gust of Wind (after Hokusai)*, and a fifth, the Marseillais popping a wheelie, who loses his cap again in the sudden shift in balance. It fell at my feet and I retrieved it. He circled the roundabout, I reached it to him as he moved past, and he took it without stopping, grinning as he approached and left our existence inside a place

glowing in the white, gold, and black of teeth missing, chipped, crooked, and crowned. In his absence the page rolled straight through summer and stretched into late the following spring the force of the evening into night lost in the calanques. Struggling for hours back along the path I followed thinking it was toward home, corner after corner opened onto the repeated

inlets created ages before when the sea-cut caves collapsed, returning the sea in them to the surface far below. Days spent searching backwards through a book, each page identical

at first glance to the one I wanted, sure to contain the longed for words even as I slowly concluded the searched-for scene, in which a choir sings in firelight on the side of a mountain to the residents of the village far below, was one I'd imagined, seemed to enclose me in its landscape of rising and falling pages. At the road where I'd continued on in error

after reading how the poet did feign that Orpheus drew trees, stones, and floods after him, I extended my thumb, then put my palms together and bent my knees, at which the driver of a white van stopped, shaking his head and laughing at the gestures, an immense presence that I, as I

stand at the faucet having written thus far, feel again as I watch the mushrooms turning over in the stream. Strange circling dots of lights were visible through the hackberry branches. After some hesitation

I took the dog to the top of the small bridge to see where two low boats in the river mouth carried large letters in electric lights mounted on a frame, $E\ A\ R\ T\ H$ on one boat and $\&\ S\ U$ on the other. The letters swayed and bobbed with the boats while on the shore a person

rotated the electric letter N in her hands like a baton. Can this continue to be true? Reading "The Book" by Bruno Schulz, I recall my last reading, around a long table in the near-dark, where it provided the founding text for a class on the making of small books. The character Signor Bosco of Milan became Prospero for us as he weighed his conclusions and "they dissolved into thin air," but it is we who dissolve, the light in the dark room growing dimmer as one of us

reads the auras of the others and I watch face after face float a few inches forward from the skulls still attached by the necks to the bodies. Another time when I arrive late, the others wait in the dark under the table (though one sits on the floor to the side and leans against the wall, the one who showed the path into the tree but did not follow it), not to surprise but to greet me in the configuration of my dreams, demonstrating their willingness to climb, as they had that night, into the pages of The Book, which I am not remembering but encountering in repetition. The dog snores, the snow balances on the power line and Daisy, Daisy whom I know to be flesh and blood, appears again in the pages as the barrel organ turns. "We shall re-create piece by piece what is one and indivisible." I walked out into the falling snow, leaving the whimpering dog behind, knowing I would talk to her and thus be unable

to hear "the shiver of fear, the presentiment of a thing without name that exceeds all our capacity for wonder" on Morrison St. just after the little free library where I stopped to read the titles—*Baby 411*, *A Practical Guide to Psychotherapy*, *Wuthering Heights*—and shivered to be in that dark room still with the presence of the people pressing me with the bodiless pressure of something not released completely as I continued reading, rather hearing, the book (The Book or the book?) in the cadence of faces and bodies not normally in alignment

with themselves or this time. "I rushed to my room. Deeply perturbed, with burning cheeks I began to turn the pages of the old Book with trembling fingers. Alas, not many remained. Not a single page of the real text," Schulz writes. "The nineteenth Autumn has come upon me / Since first I made my count,"

the poem answered in me as the room and its faces, whose names were in The Book as songs, "I saw, before I had well finished /

All suddenly mount" in rings around me. "There are things that cannot ever occur

with any precision," The Book records precisely. When the balance nerve in the vertiginous ear is severed, the vertigo increases until, after five or six weeks, the healthy ear takes over. The healthy ear hears the pen scratching on the paper, the sweaty palm lifting off the desktop, a third or fourth ear in the distribution of ears across the green land

where the small trees perceived as further away in the woodcut, the green buds on the lilac—what will happen to them? It's beginning again. The pencil sharpener is screwed into a two-by-four five inches long. It's the chrome kind usually mounted on the wall in a classroom. Eight holes, gradually increasing in diameter, circle the adjustable dial

aligning pencils of varying thickness with the three cylindrical intervolving blades inside the housing. One end of the two-by-four slopes down at a 45° angle. The other end has been cut in a gentle S curve. When a pencil is inserted, two hands must hold the board while a third turns the crank to sharpen it. The page has an *R* on it where I tested the pencil

and as I write this sentence the *R* is repeated. A dull tone comes up through the floor, tongue is noted pressing against the back of lower teeth, and the muscles, held tight, begin to loosen. A gambler is explaining the procedure he's undergone that might help me, pointing at a giant model of the inner ear I realize soon is the ductwork in an attic. He's pulling back the seals on the tubes with a poker, showing what's wrong and could be fixed, but also how they could damage the ear and make it worse. I'm holding the poker now,

not a fireplace poker but a long wooden dowel with a sharp end, the one the teacher used to indicate the countries on the map, the one of several sharing the cylinder he'd rolled down in front of the blackboard. The rubber tip that prevents damage to the surface is missing. It's my attic, I realize. I'm prying some little pieces of debris

off the tubes of the ear, recognizing them as cat food as I do, and pushing them away, wondering if an animal brought them here. Claws scratch in a dark corner and a fox's head moves into the light. Driving it back with the poker, I try to teach it (the word accompanies the action) not to come into the attic, but it keeps lunging toward me, sinking

the pointer into its side. The animal's heavier than a fox, and thicker, and snarls, perhaps a hyena. I drive the pointer further in, thinking I'm having to kill it, but it reaches me and sinks its teeth into my hand. Lying in bed afterwards, I felt that these things were happening

inside my ear, that the attic was a figure for the ear which has been troubling me by ringing or buzzing, perhaps for the same reasons that have led my father to consider having the balance nerve in his troubled ear severed, but also that the attic is not a figure but a part carried in from a story and I, as I listen

to the cicadas tintinning in the trees, accept that no sound inside is only there. Each part followed becomes a figure for the whole, and takes the others for its parts, as it is taken in turn. "Who calls so loud?" is one way of saying it. Another is: "The stage!" Another is: "Dreamed my love did find me dead." "Why do you act?" Lisa said. "It is easier than being myself," Sandy said. "And do you find that saying the words, they are your words and you

are being yourself?" "Yes, it is true, as long as one doesn't prevent it." Robert raises his head, tips and holds it, then drops it into his hands. A goldfinch sits on a sunflower, the plant bows, and the bird curls around so its beak can enter

the upside-down seed bed. The actions on the stage and the words of the characters in the play remain in the present. Smike/James extends his hand, his fingers curled, the wrist stuck in place so the knuckles touch the chest of Nicholas/Seamus, calling for his cue, though the play within

the play is over. To whom do you listen and to whom do you speak? The shadow of his hand falls onto his chest and all of us previously absorbed

in questions of order, of befores and afters, entrances and exits, in the giant ear of the theater, hammer and anvil and stirrup, we listen to the answer, stereocilia to the grounds. It was there, the tops of my feet folded below me as I listened, I saw I wanted to love the company and in the same place fear and how

this had played out in a loving of those I hadn't thought I loved and a fear, when tapped on the chest or spoken to, of being unable to respond, of being unlovable, even as those others, vulnerable or unable, I found I was not ashamed to love inside that which we hadn't fled, thee and me, and who

is Sandy, and who is Lisa, then? The small bees are swarming the sunflowers as I balance on one foot in the house and the succulent in the clay head vibrates in time with my foot and ankle, a person dispersed in the great broken ring of faces. I cannot say what I mean. The wrong words come alive, and yet they are fine hairs that break the particles into a steady stream I don't need to know. At this angle the sun divides the green ink up and down the grain and each stem of each letter includes the range of tones for which I wanted the pen to touch the paper. Hovering, it seemed closer to the book and the faces of the book that also hovered over something so near

the words without touching. A hair on the page, a hair from the hand, the green ink goes over it without making a mark or leaving any part out. A wasp descends from the gutter's lip. Some shapes are revealed by the process, some destroyed, some created, some obscured. A beetle is pushed across

the page until it falls out of the book. One of the girls in the hammock says, "I don't want to go to school tomorrow" and "Today was so sad." The sun through leaves at 7 p.m. shines

on the hammock's green cloth, making of four arms and four legs a motion from which their heads are split. "What am I? Oh my god," says one of them. I'm carrying in my palm a nest woven out of grass and milkweed floss. The breeze produced by my forward motion lifts it it floats slowly to the ground I retrieve it. "What is it?"

a child says, holding the leaf of a tree. The arrows painted on the manhole covers line up. Is the cat looking out the window? Is the dog walking down the street? Max said once we like to keep stopping to write things down and talk about them and then go back and watch them again. At this hour on the pedestrian bridge, my hand casts a blue shadow on the pink page, the color of the streetlight and the sky far off.

the other cast

Today I was sitting with these conflicts in a series

what need of one long grass with faint red seed crowns, dandelion very yellow, ragged tulips yesterday, two robins by the minivan, two yellow warblers in the catkins, a woman in a black

lace see-through housecoat over black underwear descending the stairs followed by a man in shorts and sunglasses, then both ascending smiling, the sun shining

in sandy drainage loosened time drifting by the last day in the Beach Aire at 9:23 in the morning. The left big toe throbs and

aches in neon-green socks, the left abdomen throbs and aches, each thing voluntarily on the holy antic's noun drawings, a hand cupping a penis, a tingling sensation under walking trees, and grackles opening pointed petals. The new shoots on the grapes are soft and green. I don't know where I saw a bumblebee flying in a slow straight line

a tunnel in the air that made me think of the words of an occasion place time circumference forcing their way into the alphabet. The golden robin subdued oriole golden-breasted thread puller on the long dry stalk in the stream bed of the culvert yesterday reached left then pulled right thin fibers of the dry stalk, holding each thread deep in the crook of its mouth while it pulled. Another finally flew away trailing fibers larger than its body for nest building these are good enough for writing

day year came near turns in my arms so time has friends

so in time thread is torn loose

The sun shining in my eyes speaking with Maria on the patio about her own writing, the copy of *TiP TOE SOT* I've given her flopping open on the table. She says she is making notes on puppets and soon will be talking again to her friend, a puppet maker and performer. "A ball of chicken wire or a paint rag or a discarded piece of wood or a dried lemon, may suggest to me the core of an idea for a figure," she says he said, leading me to

a conversation on the train 8 or 9 years before in which she showed how in Ben Jonson's plays acting leads to unmasking, acting shown to be a lie, producing a satiric effect that pushes the audience away, but now, continuing, she says it is also inside the lie the improviser comes alive, a link of

difference in truth to Shakespeare for whom acting is the life of life, drawing the audience close until embodiment, masked or unmasked, joins everyone present. She faced me and the receding landscape and I faced her and the approaching one. I say, (here as I wrote this the birdsong in the bush ended at the moment an oriole emerged),

It is only in pretending that the end of pretending can come, ending including the ending of acting and the ending of not acting, in poetry the ending of language and the ending of the outside of language, no cause in nature, and no cause outside either. The difference between combining and not combining falls flat where a blank concentrates. A double corona around the

moon. It looks like a daisy, L. said, walking out in her nightgown. At the party earlier the boat, full of water, floated below the surface of the water. Trembled ached breathed hovered began again nodded off began lightening began inside recalling the vision required these movements

staring down at a milkweed in the process of unfurling its leaves, the open flat flopping leaves below the curled loose thick milky (not only when it breaks) bud, how it will spread itself thin without regret over the whole landscape, exhausting preparation, what now, the lightness of the sort

felt in the shocking sudden lightness of the boats allowing the children to fall out of them into the lake whose sliminess at shore they had resisted. The sun was behind them so they were dark above the surface and a dazzle upon it. Black bee, green-and-black lizard, small butterflies with large orange spots meeting at the thorax in a yellow wing. One lands

in the road in Pioppi, I walk toward it. A car approaches and it flies away. Sky, cloud, sea, railing, sea, slats, sea and slats, framing bar, sea, concrete-

edged tile floor and sea. No sot in me or thee. Yesterday after hesitating L. went in the sea, this morning she hesitated then wouldn't come out, finally she took off her suit so the sea came in. Now we all go naked and J. dove, butt lifted high to show how L. does it. Early mountain view, silver mist shoulders

that knot human hands inside radiant places, inside perceptions. Radiant reasons, sot reasons, reasons Sot. A fly flies out the window does it

talk people almost talk when very absorbed. Handstand attempted toppled over face ass entrails each animal pigeon dove rock pigeon in the broad-leaved tree below the dovecote roars. A shovel thumps on the concrete tub. The one man in blue coveralls gives the other man in blue coveralls his plate of melanzane e peperoni after he's eaten the sausage. There are many reasons the tense changes. When a body is flat inside a wave with arms and feet extended and face down there is a rushing sound and the interpenetration of air and water in the wave energy becomes partly subcutaneous. Huge live oaks in the steep gullies pass below the roadway and continue to the sea through Japanese knotweed. Holes in the shoulder join the walkers to the flora

quilted-corner-of-eyes, contour-of-ears, tipped-toe.

Sonograms inside sounds display a split

unbecoming the sounds which weaving your song became

a twitter, a chirr, yellowing of the cloud-blue through the left window toward the east, the ridge behind Ascea that leads to Pisciotta, and then the throaty coo What do what do

I don't try to remember things from the stone floor as I lie repeating that thought very slowly dissipating. Switching to the pen with more ink and a hammer

to the east returned in fours, a human sound, not afraid of them, the sounds. F. said she imagined us going outside in the middle of the night. Lewis said,

Where are you? A dark blue line, a very flat line, Daisy, between the cloud-blue sea and the cloud-blue sky. Red starfish molecules, purple forearm-sized worm-shaped creature on the pebbles, school of tiny translucent fish, sea spider with a face on its back, quick wing flaps. Only one time exists one time in the sound of

a hammering counted through air, getting closer, reading through some ancient existence that made insects into sundials and stomach true words, loose kinship feeling so a tongue the snake a trail

the alternate world, the other cast

where people repeat the words you know

a grinder on stone. When it stops, as now, the sound of the sea returns. From the floor of the bedroom, sitting on

pillows on the blue/yellow/green tiles, I see clouds and two contrails crossing another. Max wonders what of this can be told without harm. A grinding in the stomach, a fourth contrail and the plane at its head has crossed the single one running north-south. Many days I listened to

barely existed as fate tried to come and go. We chased a mosquito around the room with a pillow, heard the bells of animals we couldn't see in the knotweed river flats. The woman who

sold us bread, marinated eggplant, cheese, sardines, and salami
was there in the evening in the only light twilight through the
propped door, the light in the grotto of Pozzo dell'uva nera where
we'd walked with these things. I handed her the eggs and yogurt,
counted out the money

thanked her, smiled, remembered the day a week later I saw her
sitting in the square chatting, one eye on the open door of the
store, the whole world propped open. An Afghan hound mounted

a yellow Lab while his red-hatted companion stood back and two
young girls tried to pull the yellow Lab away before hands on their
cheeks mouths open O O laughing retreated also. The large toad
on the promenade crossed into the flowers. J. fell on the stones as
we walked with one light along the rocky beach in the night
shadow

of the cliff. We noted other beams of light flashing out of and
inside the waves. From the balcony we saw the lights in the sea had
followed us home, green and filtered below the waves, then bright
above, accompanied by violent expulsions of air and water as the
diving spear fishermen breached

the surface and cleared their snorkels, then back below turning
circles gives hope a sustained wave of sadness at the center of this
notebook beside the knotted

waxed linen thread, the packet stitch, as I had long called the pamphlet stitch, thinking of "one put drunk into the packet-boat," an ant on the tile, each tile a face of bows and flowers seen also in the sconce with curls of iron on the wall,

but also the man sweeping the patio, white hair circling a bald head, dumping a sheet full of leaves into the woods. Ants crossing the terra-cotta tiles pause, touch,

and continue. The buzz of the inflated-pontoon boat's motor, the shout of the driver, it passes, the motor blends with another. Each rock brought from the sea on the balcony has its own shadow and some overlap. The sky is open to the sun, the door is open to the sea. A black asp or grass snake levitated through

the grass at the base of the fig tree, an outline of how not to be involved with false ideas of what was to come. Yet I tried to knock us all down where I'd been. Below the old brick bridge,

in the shadow of the new concrete bridge that flies over it, a woman threw a bucket of water on the bitter greens that rise and fall away from missing centers. A haze has almost connected

the sea and sky as L. saunters in from the porch and a fly, descendant of Bruegel's Tower of Babel in La Bibbia, makes a

series of right turns, constructing a flight path through the room
that tilts, leans

and finally topples out the door. Hitchhiking from Acciaroli,
nineteen cars passed before a man stopped for us, opened the
hatch, and shifted

three branches wrapped with bells and ribbons, bufala horn on a
chain, old military helmet. Dropping us off, he got out with us and
stood very straight in the gravel, lifted his cap four times, put on
the helmet and saluted,

a grave expression before laughing, shook my hand, and bowed to
the others. Each mountain undergirds some other mountain. The
day before yesterday or two days before that we offered

one plant after another until the horse in the field took the last
between her teeth. For thirteen days the veils beneath veils

threw you peace. Five boys and two men in an open boat,

blue trim where one boy sat at the prow, feet dangling in the
waters, splash. A couple lay on the beach ahead, below a pine
bough, in the smooth stones, she on top of him and wearing only
light-blue lacy underwear. In the narrow passing we avoided
looking but the boy reported

the woman met his eye calmly before kissing the man again. A
thousand feet up from there in Pollica we found a castle door open,
the small one set in the giant wooden one, and entered through an
archway whose crumbling fresco showed a horse and a woman

passing fruit or flowers to a missing image. The small-faced owl
barked and then flew through the hole in the living stump. Six
trunks grew from its pollarded base. I was crying as my
companions prepared to leave,

the room filled with tears and I began to sink. Have you ever
thought of saying goodbye? L. said as my entire body floated up,
lifted in its own tears, a small part of me

noting the scale, the scent, the stars reflected in the tear pool, and
also continuing inside them, the way—

and here the pen ran out of ink and I went to the counter to
borrow one. In the square men launched blue lights into the air
with rubber bands, and the lights drifted down on chutes

to the ground or back into their hands. A woman at the bar takes a
swallow then wipes her lips. Given how a day always makes new
sounds my sounds melt. This was more or less what he thought,

as the narrator says of Constance at the beginning of *Lady Chatterley's Lover* near Latina where a field of sunflowers faced southeast and the yellow petals were fringed around their green

backs seen from the train. Poetic awareness acts. Come-with-me bird whistle, waves on pebbles, stopped-dance-music, sun on terra-cotta tile reflected

an opening vowel, many consonant sounds, bright notes, and how one felt having untold sensations made direct through

a frog face fish face in the clouds, kree kree kree kree in the mouth of the swallows, the blue-and-pink crab claw dry in the sun. Thy legs stand so high

one's perceptions take in mice and single tears hold full scenes in orbit. Thou takes it too low. Trickling water tickles the hand, tells the time, the pine needle if in sun, the new impulse if already swaying

cock-a-doodle-doo. Yesterday walked, hitched a ride, walked, another ride, arrived in the dark alone, the power out. This morning over the deep clear hole in the sea, in the wonder of floating, a sudden sharp fear of falling. Sheets drip from the balcony, napkins on the trellis. I began to note the day's moments of fear,

the crushed snake in the road, boar hopping in the grass, spider in the knotweed near my face, scurry of lizards on concrete, the waving grass at the sea bottom, the sight or sound of people, asking, answering, hearing hurts not suffered diverting one's mind

and that fly bumping over and over against the screen wants to get out I didn't need to kill it. Later,

a tidal lability. In the morning the power

is still out so read *Lady Chatterley* over breakfast. Double-consciousness ends and returns, an open boat enters the harbor, glides in, the man at the helm hops out and walks to shore beside the vessel. To let myself for a minute a day a week go

missing from the golden path, was that what I feared? The shame of breaking the vibrating line between here and there resembled myself

as each scene in a play holds the dense warm flexible life of all the rehearsals and the few days or hours in a novel include all the unmentioned nearly repetitions. A man stood in the shadow of the sea wall and,

having sold one of all he'd laid out for the buyer, shook the sand from the remaining reed bags and fit them together into a single bundle that towered over him as he set out

to walk the beach again, moving slowly from the shadow into the sun. Kindred

concentration, cricket tongue, strong thump and clack of oars as a boy rows

one of the small white fishing boats past the balcony. *Composure* is perhaps a better translation of *Samadhi*

than *concentration*. It means *stand with*. To stand with the text and be present for it as one is present for the other actors, the text

a sentient being for whom I wish happiness and safety. A girl was yelling at her mother in the garden

above the entrance to this road. The mother leaned on a hoe. Water is stuck a little in my ear. An arm hair in the breeze mosquito moves through the sky. Bye bye, my eye try making all anxieties one operation. Heading down to drop the trash and shop, two white spots became a seagull when I took the reading glasses off. The alici were there in groups

inside the water. A red starfish that may have been another in

a new place I had five limbs, legs, arms, head, and the surface of the water rose and fell and I curved with it. The moonlight in the clouds had been the moonlight on the water. I was thrice the size of the light-blue car

parked at the foot of the road to Pollica. The light through the tails of the new fish, spots of blue firing in the transparent tail fin. Later I will make a sixth and final trip with trash and recycling along the rocky shore, a mile each way, six miles

full and six miles empty. A man and a woman lean back against back on the beach, not reading or speaking. Two old men pull in a net on one of the open boats. One climbs out in the chest-deep water

and walks another boat in another time to its mooring, the story more like Caliban's cry to dream again than the urge to return to the plot to kill the master and destroy his books, my own invisible spirit whispering dissension. Old Friend! In my ear I saw the snake and realized a fear of

it being complete in itself, unbranched, undivided, the whole movement of a whole body, threatening to this body divided into parts, free from the leaves of the grass and

revealed as a companion.

Thickening

Waiting for Jonathan, a five-year apprentice and now journeyman in the Plumbers and Pipefitters union, to replace the motor in the furnace, as he arranged to do during his previous visit for routine maintenance, pushing through, as he said, the replacement order while the part was under warranty, thereby preventing the failure, sure to arrive eventually because of a flaw in the design, I see the sun is making the snow sparkle where it is heaped on the bird bath and along the

lines of the honeysuckle branches and casting a blue shadow into the footsteps left after midnight in the yard by a man, though I can't say for sure if it was a man, who startled us last night as we sat with our midnight snack having come in hungry from the lake ice when his headlamp bobbed past the window a few feet from us and then paused, the beam of the light tilting up so it made the snow flash as it fell. The beam settled

on the metal cable box suspended between the branches, another visitor from the often unseen world that keeps us bound together, though unlike two weeks ago, the man did not ascend on a ladder but, seemingly satisfied with what he'd seen, turned and walked out step by step along the path of his own footsteps, as the young Hermes walked with rafts of tamarisk strapped backwards on his feet to give Apollo the impression his journey was in one direction only, and though this technician did not walk backwards, this morning the tracks appear, looking out the window as I pause in writing, to enter the yard without showing any signs of retreat, though the lights of the truck disappeared into the storm. A few flakes, seeming to originate in the clear sky, are falling from

the upper branches and flashing in the openings between the lower branches as they pass my sight line. The footsteps, the snow falling in the sun, recall to me the remark the woman made on the lake yesterday afternoon as she and her partner approached the dozens of long spokes shoveled down to the black ice and joined by our shuffling feet into an erratic circle centered on

a pile of snow I told her was going to be a snow stove. She said they'd taken it for a labyrinth, and been confused by the lack of entrance or exit. The man with her was wearing a bicycle helmet over his hat and seemed reluctant to set off when the woman suggested they walk further out. Until you can't see the shore in any direction, I added, at which they departed. Before we returned to shore, James hollowed out the interior where we planned later to build the fire. After clearing the snow from inside the dome, we saw a head-sized

methane bubble formed by the gas rising from duckweed and other organic matter decaying on the lakebed before being trapped and then surrounded by the ice that grew, as Thoreau notes in *Walden*, from the surface down. After sitting inside the snow stove, still a cave, as we hadn't yet opened a chimney in the roof, James asked me to seal him in, though later when I recounted these notes he told me he had sealed himself in by gathering

snow from the walls and transferring it to the opening, and as I continue this a day later, having been interrupted by the simultaneous arrival of Jonathan with the new furnace motor that I have just heard coming up to speed with a very slight whine sounding, as he told me it would, like a tiny jet engine, and by James emerging from his blankets, I think again about him sealed inside the snow and what I might have been

about to write in the moments I waited, facing the white dome with my camera at the ready to record his emergence, noting how the parts we'd shoveled black were white again, filled by the still more rapidly falling snow, and the strange illusion the dome offered at that moment in the twilight, its raised sides reflecting the light of the atmosphere

to a greater degree than the snow-covered lake, giving the impression that I was looking at a white road cutting through a blue-gray field, an illusion that crumbled and was transformed, as he pushed through the walled-up opening, into a still point, his red hat gathering in an instant the long road into itself. The next hours were taken up by other things. At the house after dark, we gathered bits of driftwood collected for carving but mainly uncarved, though several pieces were inscribed with lines and cross-hatchings that remind me now of the sunlight falling on the page, carrying with it the shadows of the wire screen. Our initial attempt failed,

the sticks unsurprisingly refusing to kindle from the flame of the tea lights. Despite midnight approaching and the temperature dropping, the brightness of the night—the thick clouds and snow reflecting the lights of the city from above and below allowed us to see the expression on the other's face ten feet away more clearly than we had at twilight as the snow fell or would under

a clear sky the next night—and the persistence of our intention, as so many times before, to see to completion a project begun on a whim and sure to disappear in the wind and the rain, led us to return with newspapers and thin splinters of pine he'd chopped with a hatchet in the basement, impaling his finger on one of the pieces so that the sharp end of that piece was visible in the bag of kindling by the tip marked with blood. Back on the ice, new kindling in place, the fire quickly took hold, casting a bright orange glow on him as he fed the flames through the opening in the snow, though from the opposite side only

a slight glow from the oculus and the occasional spark was visible. As the fire burned, he announced that the fish, like the three-foot-long carp we'd seen basking golden in the sun below the 18 inches of clear ice a few days before the snow had fallen, had no doubt been attracted to the light and were below us now. We stood silent for a while watching the flames, I at least attempting to invert the scene and my

point of view, to see the glow of the fire radiating above me through the ice, as a full moon or the light of a boat might appear to a swimmer below the surface at night, but also, I realize writing, as the lights we'd seen three months earlier on the prow of the boat must have appeared, the ones we initially took for the lights of a police boat searching for a body, but which were being used by bow hunters to spot and, as I thought then and now know, to attract their prey. The next day, yesterday as I write this, we returned to the ice to build a similar structure,

but larger and for ourselves instead of the fire. Stopping to inspect the intact stove and the cinders, James pulled out the longest stick, which he'd been using as a poker and one end of which, having been added to the coals, had partially burned. Inspecting it, noting how lively the blackened portion was in the purple and rose light that seemed to rise from the snow as the sun set, I told him how I'd read the sculptor David Nash's comments, in the same book where James had come across the images of stoves of snow and ice that had set us in motion, about the mystery in the transformation by fire of wood into carbon, leaving, as in the poker or any partially burned wood, the carbon

bonded to the organic compound from whose molecular bonds it had been released by the flames that produced and fed on that change, and I wonder now as I recollect the scene if he'd thought of the lines he'd spoken as Feste a few months before, "Any thing that's mended is but patch'd: virtue that transgresses is but patch'd with sin; and sin that amends is but patch'd with virtue," the burned stick being another kind of motley, akin to the one found in our brains

by the fool. As we continued further out onto the lake, toward what we imagined

to be the center, I noticed the strangely imbalanced paths we left, each marked by the broad blade of a shovel on one side, the sharp tip of a ski pole on the other, and the parallel lines of the skis between them. Turning our heads one way and then the other to make our gazes circle, and seeing no sign of the shore, we took off our skis and began to gather the snow for a cave. As we shoveled and thought

back to a conversation we'd had as we ran Act III, scene ii of *King Lear*, I taking the parts of Fool and Kent while James as Lear conversed with the storm, he asked why the lines "I am a man / more sinn'd against than sinning" had become so famous, not being, to his mind, especially beautiful. A few hours later, the snow cave raised and hollowed, with several holes

successfully patched along the way, he pushed me in head first and I pulled him in after me. Warmed by the heat of our breath and bodies, a thin film of water formed on the ice beneath us, strange on a night approaching zero. The lights of cars on the distant causeway flickered in the snow walls above our heads. Through the small entrance that seemed far away though it was just beyond my feet, the red and green lights marking the entrance to Starkweather Creek broke into

clusters of hexagons through my damp eyes or the breath frozen into crystals on my lashes. We lay for a while in silence, listening to the ice crack as if it were giving way, though it was thickening that stressed the mass to fracture.

"And"

At the end of the trail, I stood on a sea wall with one or two others and listened to C. tell a story. But at the same time, we were watching the story as he told it. The woman in the story approached us along the sea wall—spray from a wave had darkened a spot on her coat—and I said, Watch her closely and we'll understand how C. sees her. The K. we saw was not K. but his image of her taking bodily form as he told the story. C. and I sat with her at a booth in a diner. A

bearded man joined us. She was interested in him. "I'm not the one you're involved with," she said to C. "So I'm free to do what I like." I was confused, not that C. was involved with K. herself rather than his idea of her, but that his image of her was interested in someone else, that the image was the one telling him this, that his image of her knew something he did not know. I was curious to see how she was visible

in the string of initial letters and couldn't be escaped without giving up certain ideas of the sentence. I walked to the bank and back. At a sharp cry I turned toward, a loon dove under. The silhouetted coots dove under intermittently, each leaving a blank spot in the sun dazzle out of which another bird appeared. Where do you get a sense of home? she was asking. It turned out to be the strange place I already was, and not with her at all. She told me the cells of the fetus had become part of her body as her bloodstream passed through him. I was happy to be talking to her. She described writing as staying on the surface. Before going to prison we were lined up to sing an anthem,

we were heading toward death. I thought I was singing Bottom's dream to resist it but what came out of my mouth was,

> When that I was and a little tiny boy
> with a hey, ho, the wind and the rain.

Several others joined me in the song. Later in a hallway the guards were electrocuted demonstrating that the wiring was faulty and some of us escaped. The lake wave water sound arrives continuously at the rocks but in surges that rise and fall and keep one listening for a gap that never comes,

instead an awareness like the boat's water awareness, heaving, hearing the water animals, then running and feeling the weird buzz and the arm waving in concert, a second heard in the flapping page. The sun through the thinning clouds lights the drops in the two spots where the hackberry was pruned and the drops disappear as they fall toward the orange canoe. Green Henry

spotted Judith on a narrow mountain trail and she wouldn't marry him, wanting them to be free, but for twenty years when they met, once a year or daily, they were joyful. Blind drawing, singing out loud, burning candles, the upside-down canoe, he turned

and faced an opening that felt like an interior but also a public way, remembering the relation to shaping and forming letters, coming to the edge of the page, space between letters, larger space between words

to carry that outside allows the internal constructive worth of writing into the world

a complete relaxed release, a whoosh of everything, and then in that space the stories he (the grandfather) told or read had a quality Lewis finds in his own writing, a motion transferred

from one day to another, or place or person, transformed from one to another

a glint of ice in the riprap, then pendants on fibers dangling just above the water, allowing the wave peaks to touch them and the air to freeze them. Below the bluff, combs of 5 or 6 icicles had grown from the transfer of

motion, shape, and color from the small flakes to the large seed, bringing them both very close to the eye and the hand. When you don't know someone, they're the same as all the people you've ever known. When you know them well, better than anyone, you're in love with that feeling. After that, if you stick with it, you have a chance to not know them at all. And then that's a new person, maybe one of the few you'll ever meet. And so he saw the room, seeing it through the lids, feeling the light and the shapes it carried. A spider paused as it swung

in the breeze of a blanket kicked by a foot. A sudden contraction squeezed his hand and he opened his eyes and saw the same things he'd seen, multiplying and cracking in the bright sunlight coming now around the curtain and making the eyes water and turn away, then return and see.

"You have to be ready."

"What did that mean, really? What did that mean to him, and to you?"

"It meant you have to go through things. You have to be ready for not knowing what the things are going to be."

Born in 1932 and confined to her apartment, when the phone was out for a while, she almost went crazy. I told her about losing contact in Pioppi and my panic. I said we understand each other.

"The students would be chattering before class but when Merce came in everything was silent. And then after a minute he'd drop his head and say, 'And'; I'd be watching with my hands out."

She held her hands out in front of her, lying in bed, showing how she'd been ready to play.

"He made that silence. That was my religion. He was the priest."

She said playing was her meditation but she can't play now.

"I mean I could but I can't find a reason to do it."

When she got out of bed, the cord from the oxygen tank looped around her ankle and to free it she picked up her foot gracefully.

"So we're both lucky," she said, and then repeated, as I was leaving, "We're both lucky."

Through the house, a V of lake and a few lights on the far shore. The white, bright cloud in the evening sky is a reflection in the window of a white ceiling. He said he felt like he'd come loose and was flying over the surface of the earth, feathers slowly falling down from the rafters of the barn, and as I looked up at him, a reversal in which the actual memories have come to seem to be how one can sing

a refrain or refrain from doing something, his perspective changed. "This would make a good painting."

Andy's journal, 99-03: a dream, a moment of happiness seeing the arc of a drawing, the crows in the trees—

I stood up a length of driftwood so I could see its face. Seeing the white of swans I thought what day did I walk out in the dark and wonder if I heard them. It was winter it was today in late fall this morning at 5:30 a.m. in the dark the mouth of the river full of the sound of coots the moon half-moon half behind a cloud Venus the morning star very bright in the east the moon over the bridge I read part one of *Midwinter Day* after breakfast then wrote those things and others in a letter which made

the opening not sure why through which I saw those things from before, the two men with fingers curled inside palms waving floppy-fingered gloves at me and the three men unloading brick pavers from a truck the older one saying the excavation is almost finished the youngest wiping a drop from the tip of his nose. A centrifuge is used to separate varying densities the sky over there through the window mulberry hemlock is a strange blue dark but light steely blue at not even three the clouds the sun is most directly behind. We played ping-pong and the ball bounced off the patrons or flew behind the bar. No one complained. What point in your journey are you on? I said. The afterlife, she said, and laughed. Her mother and grandmother

held her hands as she died for no particular reason. She had the sense the dream would end before she died because she knew but then she did die. Poussin walking filled his pockets with pebbles, moss, grass. "It's getting dark out what's this desire?" A bibliomancy. Sitting or standing or falling

shadow of another person's arm on one's own body a secondary shadow becoming the shadow of an object on or from itself an attached shadow the body is peopled with shadows a white-gray light flickers in the green-brown sidewalk puddle where the agitation of the raindrops picks up the gray sky light another figure entering the space of the body of water that is already persistence of

the concentration sliding through felt ground. It was as if the first time around the outline

the letters were an idea and the second time a thing, a present. It is in a moment of simulation that something uncanny comes to life though I can't find the citation and instead the letters well and burst, or walk away. The snow melts and continues to melt as it reaches the ground warmed by yesterday's rain. I'm in a very long line

with many others hoping to certify in some way ourselves as citizens. I'm told each person must sit with one of the spies to be certified. There are four empty chairs at the table. "I guess the spies are all undercover," I say, though it seems a little dangerous to be joking. Walking away with a young girl, 8 or 9, I am trying to help her answer the questions required of all of us: Name a person who was recently killed and another one

you can't remember. I say, "What happened in Charlotte? In Squirrel Hill?" "Lamentings heard i' th' air, strange screams of death / And prophesying, with accents terrible," burst from her. I didn't understand but she said she'd explain. The muskrat threw itself into the creek then ducked under violently again when it surfaced and found me waiting. Discarded two yellow kale leaves and cooked four green ones. What does friable mean? Fragile instead of labile. The light falls on three pebbles and five blue pills

Three hundred tiers of green hills above the valley

Serious tones in the house's foundation

Last night in the ski lodge I danced while I wrote and the snow-making machines reflected in the pond flung the snow deep into the earth and the secret language of direct address lifted spirits. Being in a room with others in this case allows a person to write, to hear writing in listening, and make writing as listening. Or running, running into the kitchen to check the onions I knew were burning suddenly knew but were only cooking, softening, becoming translucent and pliable, the essence of the feeling "Lila is typing..."

James said everyone knows what's in them but I said it would be different to see them written down all together. They're at the house in the country

and Lisa is showing me a sheet with printed numbers crossed off in pen. "We've had 99 root beers over the years," Lisa says, meaning she and James. Lisa and I are walking through a field. At a muddy spot I start to go right, she urges us to the left, and I sink into the boggy grass shouting. We both take a step or two and fall flat on our faces in the water

pooled between the ground and the grass tips. Her forehead, she points out as she rises to her knees, landed directly on a grassy ball of dung. We lift the clear water in our hands and splash it on our faces. The geese on the lake run on the ice and begin to separate from their cast shadows. Three stand, having landed on the edge of the ice, and the bodies attached to the shadows make sideways Ws that show black against the long yellow plane of ice behind them. The constellation of holes where the water drained through the ceiling painted with stars and connected with lights suggests a bird, a flower, a boat. Skin licked

under a window draws the clouds in and pushes the hand in closer. Sometimes opening isn't light but the observation down below the aura, tufted titmouse repetitions over the bog, knotted wood, grass, answer plainly. Peaceful and distracted, distracted without knowing it, distracted by distraction (distraught), head off, though I don't recall moving it, strong inner awareness then an external sense of straightening the dark flecks in the white underside of the peregrine falcon,

the grass coming through snow below it. Ice pushed together by the wind made a thin cracking sound. Triangle print of a wedge-heeled shoe going down a hill made me listen. A small girl in a park brushes snow off a wall with her mitten, how changing

the way it looks feels day after day in the long road back to the present under thoughts of dying or being dead and punctuated by moments of great emotion, a large box, 6' × 4', with a cover attached to a rope at four points, the cover to be thus lifted off and show the character reborn. "No-oh, no-oh," the director said to me. The most important thing, the intention and the vow, is not to know what was going to happen before it had happened, which takes the form of not talking to certain people who claim these visions of the future. A man left singing from

a large bar, as apparently he did every day, that life was wonderful. Someone walked by carrying a statue or object in which a singing bowl, singing as it passed, was held aloft by four birds. Someone said, This really is the most magical place, as if a vote were being held and it was sure to win. I was holding a parking space for someone by standing in the street, someone I knew but couldn't place. The woman who held the temptation of knowing things before they had happened also seemed to be a series of lights set at intervals around a wire tucked into the molding. The letter carrier started across the road, glanced at a letter in his hand, then turned back and delivered it to the house he'd just left. One came inside with horror,

counting, measuring, weighing, earning an advance. The physical act of writing tenses the tensing muscles around the right kidney and the crown of the knee lifts the page a fraction of an inch. A rainstorm sinks into the stone and emerges far down a sheer face having traveled through an internal fault in the rock. We never arrived

we will never arrive there the poem sounds like that or also icy
another week of black ice every morning

tripped over the orange boat dragging the yellow boat over the
grass after the open water along the edge of the ice

Swans with tongues came waddling along, peacocks, woodcocks,
marsh wrens. The wings looked like a divan. The palate loosens
and the air passes through the neck to the back-body and what is
beneath it, what he could not have described, the ribs and soft
tissue knitted together, the capacity for expansion and contraction.
The sources of suffering move. He remembered the one in

Brooklyn, age four. There was a fire in the stove and it was put
out with flour, which he was fascinated by and so kept telling
people, There was a fire and they put it out with flour. They took
the subway home while some stayed to help. He remembered he
was crying and then stopped and was sad that the stuffed rabbit in
the apartment hadn't seen him crying. She told him the rabbit
would be able to tell he had been crying. He wondered why he had
wanted the rabbit to know. It feels much better now

than it did before. The Greenstreets are visiting us in a large loft
apartment. They are going to go out in the car for the day and
maybe will not come back for a second night, as it is a three- or

four-hour drive to where the trees they want are crusted in salt in
the desert. They say it's too bad they won't return, they only need
to re-record the one word, "scar," that couldn't be heard in my line.
F. suggests we could record it here with our equipment. Later she
tells me they explained it

was a failure because I brought a whole world into it. "I
overacted." "You acted." I felt for the difference between them.
Another time, we saw the

whooping cranes floating in the river, not flying north. In knotting
the I, one myth about Blake's wholly line joining all beings,
grinding her in him in a lily garden or rathole a radio radio-like tree
plopped behind choke-cherry hill. At dusk a muskrat pursued a
mallard in a tightening spiral until the mallard swam off in another
direction. A small guitar sounds farther away than a large one. A
few flakes continue to fall. It has often happened

to me that when I ask did you say my name? The other person says
no I didn't say anything. What's that like, to be able to hold a
sound and make another sound until the two sounds fit? To have
the sensation of choice? I have tried but the held sound changes to

the one I hear. It shifts and the right sound is the one that's
happening and there is nothing to compare. Or so I've thought, but

the songs I've sung a hundred times, sung and heard, when I strike the wrong chord

in those I hear the difference and look at the sheet of chords or even find it on my own by trying one and then another. I still can't find them from nothing. At midnight we stepped out onto the porch to mark the year's passage and blew several blasts on the trumpet. But there are also breaks within things. A single thing

has many sections. I thought one might confuse these kinds of division, the divisions between things and the divisions within things, but after a moment a thought came to me and I said it. "You could

add, 'The reverse is also true,' for I believe the breaks between things are also breaks within things and the breaks within things are also breaks between things and the simultaneous and exchangeable nature of divisions internal and external is one of the subjects of the book and also one of the great subjects of poetry, a state of things that is, as Olivia says, of the beloved doubled, 'Most wonderful!' One does not preclude the other! All writing," I concluded, "is and might be

a single thing divided within and many things divided between." I was smiling, laughing, almost giddy with excitement and the pleasure of the conversation and its discoveries. She, while giving a look of sadness and happiness and sorrow and wistfulness and anger and patience and love and pity and boredom and exasperation, nodded slowly and said, "No," and as I pursed my lips to begin talking, no she said no, don't know, thanking me for the words, but no, sitting on the daybed to continue the work from which she had just taken a break to open and eat the fruit and seeds of a pomegranate, the first of the year.

Cia ao ao ao ao ao ao

I slid the mattress off the sagging bed to sleep on the floor of
Hotel Mondial. The metal cot springs stretched across the
empty frame

below a black-and-white photograph printed on vinyl that
had the texture of canvas but lacked a weaving's warp and
weft, presenting instead a single surface. A man stands at the
stern looking down at the line where the oddly tilted boat is
trapped

in ice I took at first to be water solidified by the photographic
process. The floor, which bore the image of a rattan mat's
coarse weave, was smooth below bare feet. The sun rose on
the terra-cotta roof of a stucco house across the way. A dog
slept in the shade on the front porch. The bus climbed, the
weight gave out of the body the mountains

to stay in the letters swimming in the ether. A bird with
yellow head and tail flew up a stream. Gnats appeared in the
swallows' flight patterns. A cloud descending Terza Piccola
had one crawling on its goat face halfway down the
overlapping pines where the glass intervenes. It evaded my
attempts to release it, passing close to the

nose, dotting the eye. A thousand days ago my back spasmed.
I could hardly walk and the rearview mirror came off in my

hand when I tried to adjust it. I'm typing one notebook, noting what I find in another. Women outside or in the building begin to converse and the voices are full of energy I can't put words to. A bus driver, blue official shirt

open four buttons, silver hoop earrings, bulging arms, and tattoo of a tree with a heart in its roots, directed me to wait here for the bus that is sure to arrive subito. It pulls in, he walks over and speaks with the driver; an off-duty driver hitching a ride; and a young man with four feathers

in his small hat, a carved walking stick, large silver rings on his fingers, wide pants short of the ankle, soft suede boots, many thin necklaces. We'd passed each other in the street earlier. The one who showed me the way steps off, our driver reaches for the switch and starts the engine. Walking later

the young man pauses in San Pietro, glances at me without recognition on the bench where I'm writing, and shouts to the occupants of a slowly approaching Alfa Romeo. A bass line shakes the car, cia ao ao ao ao ao ao ao, he says, loose clothes and ribboned stick, beads, and hat feathers vibrating sympathetically as he climbs in beside the sharply-dressed couple, slinging in front of him the backpack. The steel cup that hangs from it on a short chain clatters against the door frame. In the new room, I didn't read the letter again, not wanting to be seen. Wet clothes smelling of rose from the cheap detergent, unrinsed by the broken machine, are dripping on the balcony. A red dot on the fuse box flashed. What's the English word for that? Ivana said. A fuse, I said, a fuse box. The bells at 8 p.m. are ringing. The tongue hits the bell and the bell vibrates. Speaking or reading or thinking or gentle or violent so

often I attempt to conceal. The handhold came loose and rolled down the scree field. During a brief heavy rain, the white horse in the field across the river stood stiller than the grasses thrashed by the storm. Then it was led to shelter. I saw this. I didn't want the person to arrive as I was singing

the alignment of the body, allowing its shapes and patterns to emerge. 30 feet away the wings of an insect beat against the air. "Ciao," I said, and the proprietor's face glowed as she said "good bye." The strange word became two words and I saw the pleasure they gave

her mouth as it opened and closed again. On Saturday, she told me, the large loaves come. At 4 a.m., I rolled away from the half-moon and onto my left side where in my heart beating heavily against my ribs I felt compressed. In fear and discomfort I rolled back to where I'd been and let gravity draw my heart's beating away from perception. The shirt drying in the window twists right then left in the breeze. The river changes color, clearing to mint green and white, clouding to a uniform tan, not at the moment of a storm, but near the end or minutes or hours after. The old neighbor pinched her thumb and forefinger to her lips, drawing through them a hissing breath, then flapping her hand to disperse the smoke that wasn't there. No, I said sorrowfully and as she continued speaking I realized she was not asking for a cigarette but if the clouds

had issued from my mouth. Io non fiume, io capisco piccolo. The guitar rests across two chairs, unplayed in the shared house. Today will change these thoughts. A wall of moss on a garage lintel, caves and overhangs two inches tall, green and ochre, stems with yellow flowers three times higher. *Non vietato*. After a loud knocking, I stood up from meditation and answered the door, but it was on another

floor, in another sound. Dandelion greens picked and held over the fence didn't draw the two donkeys down the hill. Ivana's father reached out through his kitchen window to shake my hand. I was passing on the road. English makes my mind wander, he said slowly. Taking in the laundry, the time I dropped it off a balcony 33 years ago in Pisa on my way to Assisi to see the cell of Francis where the threshold stone was worn to ankle-depth and I looked down in the same long way to my T-shirt on the roof came back to me. The walk up the hill from the train station with tourists and pilgrims has been a terrain of arrival in dreams where the group of people slowly separates as they walk, attaching to

a memory before it can be completed. In Assisi my room, the cheapest available, barely wider than the single bed, reached so high I seemed to be at the bottom of a well. Clouds reflected in the single window

leaning inward floated out of reach below the ceiling. On the bed eating tuna from the can with bread, running out of lira, I was among the images. Outside the basilica I stood and read descriptions of the tiny reproductions, including the *Ecstasy of Saint Francis*, in which he is lifted into the sky on a cloud the text named a flaming chariot. The frescoes had been damaged by the earthquake and couldn't be seen directly. In many garages here sophisticated machines in gray cases used to grind lenses wait beside stacked bags of crushed pumice. A short axe struck a small log and five gentle blows

against the block before it split, whereupon the man rested the hatchet in the block again, bending down to pick up the two new pieces, adding them to the stack of thousands beneath a three-sided shelter. A pipe from the hillside diverted one of the many streams or springs into a cistern, filling it to the height of an elevated drain, keeping the basin full and the excess running down the slope to the river. Often a knot one records will lapse, sliding toward the

mountains, the wreathing clouds, the evergreens' smell, the sound of the river, but the heavy center of the mind keeps cursing, the body contracting. A skinny boy adjusts his yellow pants as he takes off on a dirt bike. Two boys play soccer with a pebble and the larger one kicks it hard into the curbstone. A clunk follows. A girl walks out of the shuttered house and another in an orange Fiat beeps the horn. Seven posters commemorate men recently deceased, including long-haired Sergio Zampul, who shares a name with my host Ivana. He raises two fingers, a peace sign in the shallow sun, last hour for hour's recognition

the declining will allows someone through. The bee accompanied me for a few steps in the morning. Terza Media appeared through the trees, birds sang far off, a bell rang nine, a dog barked. Six hours later I laid my body in the moss. A fly inspected my ear and found it empty, did not bite the ankle, and then it was time to go. Another fly

pollinated a white flower smaller than itself as I crept down
the sandy wash I'd taken for the path, turning around at a
cliff's edge. Heaving myself up until I rediscovered the way,
out of breath, heart pounding, I stuck my head in a pool of
snowmelt and the walls of the valley

pressed against my face through the sheets of water. It's quiet
now on the balcony. Lingering naked in the torrent, I missed
the chance to offer myself to the one car descending the
closed road and walked into a great tenderness for the small
larch by the guardrail, the pines surrounding it, the leaves of
the arnica, the red and white ribbons that blocked the
short-cuts, preventing erosion between

eight successive hairpins. A man—we smiled to one
another—ascended on a motorbike. Many swallows in front
of the pines curve more gently than in the evening. What
passeth acknowledgment

will in co-lamentation come otherwise, dialogues from
unknown narratives and other bits of talk radiating their
thoughts or plans, closer to dreams. Karaoke by the river.
Kids played soccer

where picnic tables had been pushed aside and adults sang or
stood beneath the tent and listened. I can see the col I went

over, one of many ridges. Max asked if this time will be part of the fiction and how to give the man in the past his errors as perceptions and for the first time voices in the house were drifting into the room, disturbing, stirring up

these ruminations. I opened the window and the sound of the river filled the interior with its rushing and dissolved me in a measure where *difference* and *machine* and *sidewalk* and *know him* rhymed in the singer's mouth, the lineaments forgotten. Wild strawberries, small and sour, where my foot went through the moss between the roots. Enjoy being back on Earth, F. said somewhere. A woman at the bus stop in Santo Stefano, her spine curved sharply

forward, was baffled by an automated voice I heard also. It didn't answer her questions but kept repeating options I couldn't understand either. Lowering the phone, she said to me, Santo Pietro? and then led me to the smaller bus I hadn't taken before, marked Contralta, as the voice on the phone continued. Three men are clearing the hillside with weed-whackers. A single chain saw. I saw through my lids into the bright

cube of the room, but the objects didn't appear. Some of his sufferings have fallen away from me, some continue, but I judge myself and others less harshly and individual figures of mist twist and turn

settle down now say things are closed.

I made an exception to see the bird that was tuttering shaded from the sun and the bride was two trees over brown orange rust pine straw feathers and a red beast very so often the tut rises into fluting high note. I wondered if the Buddha gives examples of when to open the eyes in meditation or

otherwise interrupt gnats crawled in my ear and on my cheek I didn't look following the river up from the waterfall having climbed above it in the woods a few hundred strides up the gorge the stones became dry and I saw the water flowed from two holes below a few times the size of my throat many times

I had heard that bird but it never came close until I sat still with eyes closed. There is a waterfall inside the key inside and another one inside the W after all itself meant there is a waterfall inside the body inside the waterfall and another waterfall inside the waterfall itself the needles if the tiny pines I'm sitting in are soft I started walking the other direction to the waterfall clouds small rips through the boughs a cloud of mist like the ones I've been watching from the balcony filled the forest doors the emptiness the sign-less the wish-less

the buzz of the weed-whackers below the window

and the six men are gone. Last night reading *Women in Love* in the evening I glanced out the window and saw the rainbow and climbed out to study it. The neighbor who shares this floor with me raises her shutter with a grinding sound. The first day I cranked and wedged the ones in here

to stay open the last two inches. A child is calling for Mr. Meier and I get up to answer. He is at the bottom of the wide stairs on the landing between floors. I go down to see him. He's very upset. The devil is going to make me watch an execution, he tells me. I take the boy's hand and a man appears, balding, dark hair, staring at us with a sneer. I stand tall, lean towards him. "I see you motherfucker." As I tried to return, I wanted to lie on my left side and face the wardrobe. The devil's not in there

I said to myself very clearly, but still I didn't want to turn my back on the doors until my heart pounded with such physical presence against my ribs I couldn't bear it and turned my back on them. I thought of Māra disappearing when named, but to have this dream of confrontation by clear sight,

I'd gone to a place I couldn't be recognized. What had I turned away from? How did that bind me to what I'd called out? I spoke to the goatherd on the way to the waterfall and then again on the way down. He was in almost the same place, descending again, so I came down through the new flock behind him. Two goats clashed horns then broke apart and looked at me calmly. One in five or six had a bell. He told me he milks them for formaggi di ricotta. The sensation of running up the river rock by rock, landing on what was there without thought, continued in the curve of the boulder below my spine in the center of the rapids and the underwear wet from swimming under the hat on which I rested my head, the roar of the river

in the thus audible breath. The boys downstairs hoot like owls. At Fiori|Pane, the young woman asked where I was from, then why was I here. She widened her eyes. "That's wonderful." When I write

"she said," who dares to laugh? To whom do you speak freely? One small cloud full of sun shifting in place above the pines of Terza Piccola acts as a lens, casting a white light on the section of trees that becomes a grove. I searched for and missed

the little hum of fear my body bore in Pioppi. The flare of a thought appears in the skin of the face, the nerves of the fingers, and is never to be understood by a person in the room who observes it or the person having it. A physical sensation precedes and follows the petal being that told its tale directly. The towering human, maybe once the action of the play,

had caused me to look directly into the eyes of Seamus, then in another play into Olivia's, and the angle of the stage lights and my extreme proximity showed me how things I had previously seen as one floated separately in the globe of vitreous humour. A sudden breeze releases a cloud of pine pollen. A fly on

the knee glistens in the sun. The drops from the cascade fly out of the shade into that light. The stone pine sprawls across the top of the huge boulder across from us, me and the fly, the sun touches the edge of the cliff, and the temperature drops. When I opened my eyes, sensing more than the time had passed, the gorge, pine, boulder, and distant mountain vibrated, a gong whose sound is visible while appearances are still, being in several places at once. I rubbed my left thumbnail on the page for a while instead of writing. The bus driver said the name of a person warmly to the couple across from and just behind him. "Morto," said the man. "Mio professore di Italiano," the driver said sadly, shaking his head. "Grazie,"

I said as I exited the bus, acknowledging my place in the story, and began to climb the winding road to Val Visdende. A yellow ball caught in the eddy of a torrent circled under an overhang. Eventually, though nothing seemed to have changed, a trapped log, spun by the current, pushed the ball into the sun, where it bobbed in the roaring water. The eddy soon brought it under the overhang again. I climbed until I counted the 23 petals of a yellow daisy, mountain arnica, and watched it

flutter, tethered by its stem. For a split second it reflected the sun's rays into my eyes. Spiders hung limp at the end of long threads, becoming two bees hovering as my eyes cleared. Rain clouds touch the mountain two valleys over. The river a thousand meters below my boots is in the sun. Must everything be openly discussed? Max was driving me to their place in a car. We met Kate and she showed us a painting.

Max said the left shoulder blade was not good, it was upsetting, looked like a wire was showing through. Kate thought it was fine, she looked nice, the woman in the painting

with the wire showing through, and I agreed, but then when I glanced out, the neighbor girl, maybe 12 or 13, stood on the balcony next door looking at her reflection in the window, and I felt my lack of skill in witnessing these solitary moments. She straightened her neck and raised her chin, studied the result. I hoped she didn't know I saw, didn't think she did. Beginning as a way to validate what had happened,

it becomes a who, allowing contentment. In the shadow of a rock where I swam, a large trout hovered. A man moved slowly down the river in rubber waders. He seemed to be floating, looking for a place to cast his line. I held my hands a foot apart and pointed to the place at my feet. He shouted and motioned that up the river there was a

pool where I could dive in, miming the action. I didn't want him to catch the fish, so why give the signal bearing the English noun "here"? On the bus began to cry, in the wake of this and last night and the morning's loss to agitation in the presence of new neighbors who just now shook the floor again coming or going. The reaction to such slight interruptions was the minute-to-minute fear returned. I stopped for a moment to look but I forgot to breathe in one place among the pools and streams where the water pulsed clearly out of a hole in the ground. A distance one may feel soars above death. The gray heron landed in the river. The two white spots

on its wings were lost when folded, but nearer to the rushing water than before. A girl with an owl on her arm limped, had difficulty speaking, and asked a stranger to move over so she could sit beside her on the nearly empty bus and frequently her bare shoulder where the owl was inked leaned against the stranger, who at first angled toward the window to make space but then sat straighter, more upright, and accepted, no, in truth received the touch. Palm, pinkie and parts of

other fingers rest on thickly-inked upside-down words. A creature of fog unfolds, rising and expanding, looking me in the eye from its cat head, and fading away. The last thing is a dark-green pine, high and alone in a grove of larch. The pulsing in the low back

taken in from the room and the river, repeated from the Beach Aire, revealed part of a sequence, as the support hand's movement to various parts of the notebook and page reveals the words in sections, but when I woke in the night to back spasms and pain seeming to confirm that I was sliding toward the state I was in before I left, as has been true many nights, the mist outside the window, through which the parts could be seen clearly, including the mist, brought tears to my eyes also. The mist blocked, shifted and was gone though the wall and a corner of the pillow continued for

now to block sections of the mountain. High above the torrent, I sat beside the path in sun then clouds, hat on head and red kerchief on neck, leaning against a rock. Solitary larches and pines rooted in the scree flow held the path upright. A blue insect met for the first time sat long on my knee as if it knew I wasn't allowed to leave. Lying in the gravel above the river valley, ant on chin, I bathed in the chain saw surges, losing the sentences. I saw the goal was outside who is

silent and who is speaking. Two men held an angry discussion. Several times they wiped their bare, sweating heads with rags. One began to clear a row by walking

straight down the hill and swinging the weed-whacker in front of him, while the other continued to clear in curving lines that matched the contours of the land, sometimes widening his cuts into shapes that seemed not to have their source in the terrain. The swallows swooped above the men to eat the insects disturbed by the clearing,

a new moment. The whine rises as the man squeezes the weed-whacker's throttle. When he lightens his touch, the monofilament snapping through individual stems is audible. The owl lighter, lost until today, rhymes with the tattoo on the girl's arm. One tuft of grass in the gravel quivers, each blade

moving in a slightly different signature. The woman who asked if she could park by the recycling bins where I was descending to the river touched my left breast when I said I was American and read out slowly the word her finger touched, *Patagonia*, first contact in a month beyond a few handshakes. Each day is alive in an undying way, even as its participants, the actors in a play, are themselves dying. The performance is singular and the day is available and will be performed again tomorrow, the touch radiating in my chest, a geranium petal rolling over twice, inside outside inside, across the cobbles. Two women are sitting with me

they aren't waiting for the bus they are across the street at *Milk & Coffee*, the name painted blue on the wall above them, below the banner *Prodotti Tipici*, drinking bitter orange spritz

with potato chips. The woman on the right touches her glass
salut against the glass on the table while the hands eyes body
of the other woman are occupied by the screen

the song again disguised as another but when will it be a new
song and will I know

let in no more light than the white net fence meant to keep
the skiers out of the chasm but providing entrance and exit
for the sound of the water by piercing here and there the
walker's trance-like summer progression. Slipped off a high
clod, floated over two white spherical mushrooms. The fly
on my leg walks and touches with its proboscis the weave of
the fabric and the groove of the zipper

How quickly love appears

not wanting to miss the bus again, looking up at each
car-passing sound, that woman walking past had a flower in
her ear. Va bene? she asked, leaving the library with her
children. I opened my eyes saw my hands formed a circle in
my lap the fingertips touching. Bene beautiful good okay.
The younger neighbor

behind a bush on her bike on the high side of the road edges
out.

"Do you like chickens?"

"Yes, I do." I have seen both girls embracing the birds. "You speak English?"

"No," she says forcefully, stepping back into

the leaves, but one focuses on the words so clearly, lovingly, with such articulation and experience of the sensations of the words that one joins them where they are, as if one were memorizing a situation or landscape, attending to it with great focus, a body involved in going up the hill in two languages to not slide off the cliff to hear the word from the bush and in that effort the writing is unified, the loose free light writing coinciding and sharing with the body what might otherwise be called distraction or digging out from under

a throbbing compressor somewhere in the building shuts off. Up the stream I sat on my heels in the thunder, attracted by the five levels of the forest, trees to left and right, moss-footed pines, log-fringing moss, tight tiny ferns, orange dried needles, familiar clover, and plants that rise a few inches on a narrow straight stem that branches three times, each branch three-leaved, a hollow at the center in a sudden anxiety in the myriad details how will I and everyone move from here to there and there to near, and find each other, what will I carry on and what will I leave, how much will it cost

who will bear the price. The clouds are very dark and the noon bells are ringing. As I walk up the hill with bread, milk, beer, vegetables, the swallow songs seem new, echoing off the school building. Certain motions triggered

the fear it was hard to remember what it is like the cloud moving through the larch without being torn apart. "Yahoo," the girl is yelling, "chick chick choo." The bird watches her. The rain begins to fall at a slight slant, a slant slightly different from the trees that lean a few more degrees into the mountain.

There's the trampoline doing flips and there's the small girl who did them doing them and when I widen my eyes in appreciation she does another Wow I say she laughs and does a third and continues as I drift out of sight up the street to write this on a bench beside the fountain faucet below *Fermata a richiesta* the drops melting and spreading the stem of some letters the clouds in the needles doing the same leaving

a droplet in the green between space of vision and the
present encounter with pink small lilies on tall stems by the
river I will name you later

time will change shape. A small dog barks, an old man veers
into the street half-squatting, shirt-tails flapping, zooms away
in a white Fiat. Waking in the night with heart fears after ear
pain I rolled left. It has never been pain, the writing says, that
makes me move

but an awareness normally avoided that is at the root of
panic. The mist wall broke into individual shapes large dog,
dragon, two eyes colliding in a fish. The sun showed the wind
circling a web, the wind showed the sun. I will sit on the
ground and try to hear a little of what he is saying. What
does it mean, what is the use of filling one thing with others?
I cannot do it, yet my right eye twitches, third

middle right toenail is fuchsia from hammering it out
repeatedly against the inside of the boot. Once like rejoicers
we were transcribed. Imago mundi,

in the casement of the open window I sat and read
Shinobu-moji-zuri, name of the rock. It is derived from the
green grain used to take a rubbing said to show the face of
one's beloved. The verb form, the name of the village, means

to recall times past, to conceal oneself, to endure. The rock is half-buried now, toppled in olden times to prevent tourists digging up the likeness-making grasses. Kids tumble out of

the yellow house in a chasing game, circling and returning. A swallow swerves inches from the book, and the girl in gray sits under the eaves with her face in her knees. The boy in blue leans against a barrel, the neighbor's duck walks down the plank connecting its green-roofed house to the wet grass, and at the bottom of the hill a boy in an orange shirt dances in his driveway as a person in the doorway calls him in. Hovering over this gorge a golden eagle

balanced on the funneled updraft in the fine adjustments of wings and body, the shifts in posture, stance, and tone that allow the forest and mountains to remain around the narrow confluence where rivers gather and drop down the next breath, the clouds moving very fast with loose fine dangling edges followed by a fluid turning head. A small island of stone appears. The water hits and divides and

the downstream half harbors a plant with small white-and-yellow flowers, green and ochre moss sparkling with drops, and vibrating grasses. In the chasm, the two mountains, kilometers apart at the peaks, stand at arm's length, joined by the stream become a torrent that appeared and disappeared as I descended the path along the cliff, one of all the narrow ways I had traveled to arrive here through vast, smashed and eroded structures, down which slowly or quickly I was borne and stumbled. The forest is blurry through reading glasses. Hum bees hovered three or four a foot above my head barely moving

bathing me in the humming sinking closer and closer. Three times I looked and they retreated as my eyes closed again. Kneeling instead of lying, when I swayed a little it floated on the spine, the head ahead or behind like the lotus blossom on a long root in the spring-fed lake clearly moving a year before as we paddled toward the Crystal River. An asp crossed the greenery of the cow path

I'd mistakenly followed. Hops and leaps. Two mushroom seekers pointed to the descent and in the field of cabbage green a heavy sound of chirping frogs or crickets not to know until there and then react gently. A black-and-white grouse burst out of the ground cover near Campolongo. I don't remember the dream except the sensation of a real thing side by side with its simulation

is haunting me as I walk beside the river. A thin aspen balances on one leg between the pines. Tonight more of the moon will be visible and more of me and more of the mountain. Eyes closed, shade of a trunk,

clouds passed in front of the sun. Tomorrow at noon I will
begin descending to sea level. When I read it I thought, He's
happy. He was anxious and now he is OK. Having done these
things to the tune of these myths are ways of working one
has faith in. A sharp, human whistle and the train begins
rolling. A bag labeled *People's Republic of China* found
half-buried in sand

in the river, silt and the sarcophagi of river flies wiped off,
carries these notebooks into the present. I thought I must
look different. I imagined Lisa saying, You are floating. I
imagined floating and felt floating flood the visible. It's day

but all the shades are closed. In and out of tiny silences the
pitch and yaw move the body a few inches from itself and
then return it to the outlines. This too makes a sound.

A crab apple on the tree in the milkweed forest and the dwarf
bald cypress

grown into a human shape. Orange twine holds the milkweed
back and the pumice hive sits on a red cushion in the sun.
James says his Richard II is sadder

than the other actor's, for no thought is contented. A woman
walking past disappears behind the milkweed. Socks hang on

the line above the cacti. The larch is thriving. The #3 bus
passes and the porch shakes. No self is in control of
emotions, thoughts, everything in

the body, et cetera, the trees, the weather, the cities, the
birds. Let's say you can't remember which drawer your shirts
are in or which way to turn when you get out of bed, a white
van, a black car, two sparrows chase a buzzing grasshopper
into the porch and one catches it. Andy's cancer has spread
to his hip and spine and his sister, my mother, Carrie, who
found out Tuesday, is coming today to visit. Every day for a
year, since his first diagnosis, they have talked on the phone,
discussing the plays of Shakespeare, scene by the scene.

Acknowledgments

A Companion, and its companion, *A Duration*, are dedicated to the memory of my uncle, Andrew M. Johnson.

"'And'" is for Pat Richter, pianist, composer, and Merce Cunningham's "one and only studio pianist . . . whose marvelous tunes put a supportive sound floor under generations of dancers who loved her." www.youtube.com/watch?v=0DF-4Cs1bvM

Thanks to the editors of *Allium* for publishing earlier versions of "An ideogram for our descent thus far" and "'One of those open fields . . . shaped like ears'"

and to the editors of *ZAZA* for publishing an excerpt from an earlier version of "An indefinite and expanding time."

My gratitude to the many people, animals, and things in whose presence and absence I found the composure and composition of this book.